The James Tiptree Jr. Award

Space Babe Coloring Book

Jeanne Gomoll

Introduction by Ellen Klages

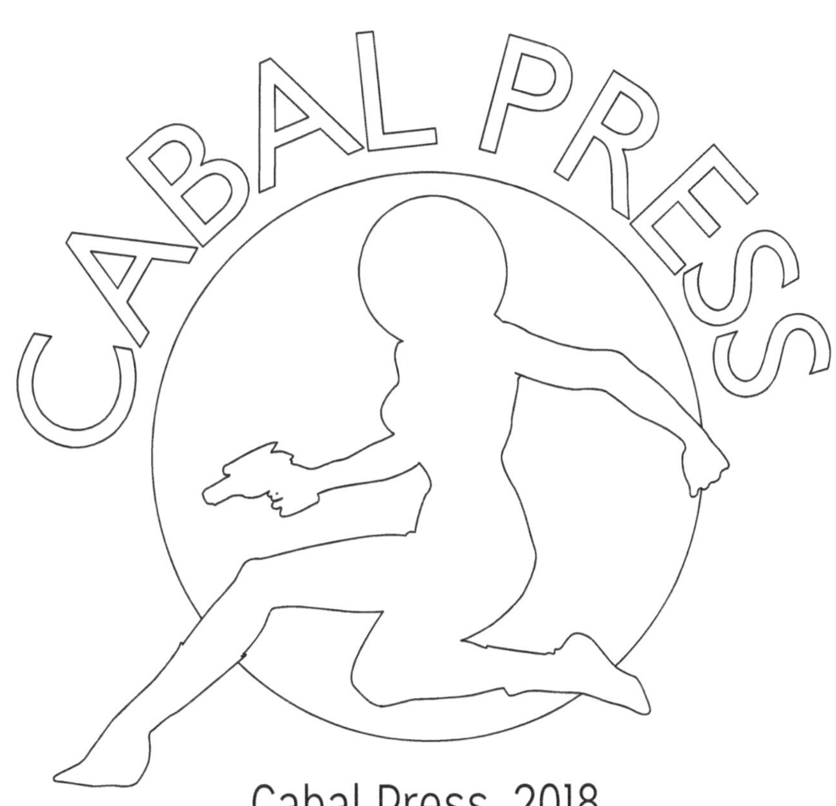

Cabal Press, 2018

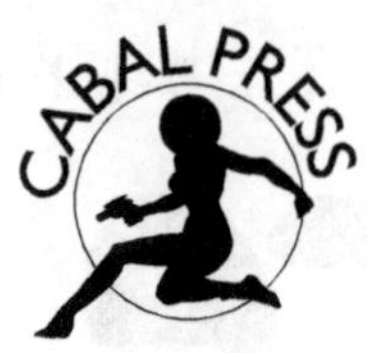

Cabal Press
Info@Tiptree.org

Illustrations and book design by Jeanne Gomoll
Union Street Design, LLC

The Space Babe image (front cover) is the registered trademark of the James Tiptree Jr. Award.
Based on cover art for *Fantastic Worlds*, #7 by John Celardo (Artist not confirmed), January 1953

ISBN 978-0-9994998-1-8

Special WisCon Edition
First Edition

Acknowledgments

*It was Ellen Klages's idea that the James Tiptree Jr. Award needed a Space Babe tattoo in 1997.
And it was Ellen's hilarious and brilliant performances and the auction items she created for Tiptree auctions, that helped to popularize Space Babe, and made the image synonymous with the James Tiptree Jr. Award.
Thank you, Ellen.*

I also want to express my appreciation to micha cárdenas, Ineke Chen-Meyer, Elizabeth LaPensée. Alexis Lothian, Anna-Marie McLemore. Pat Murphy, H. Pueyo, and Isabel Schechter for their suggestions and feedback on the many faces of Space Babe.

F. J. Bergman came to my rescue when I cried out, "I need a poet!"

Debbie Notkin gave me some essential publishing advice.

Jeff Smith and Pat Murphy helped me proofread this book, a service for which we should all be grateful; let me assure you.

*I wish I could also thank my Dad for the words of wisdom he offered me many, many years ago—
"You need to work on your hand-drawing skills!" (Better now, Dad?)*

And lastly, I want to express my love and gratitude to my partner, Scott Custis, for his encouragement, suggestions, and support.

– Jeanne Gomoll

*Dedicated to my sister Julie, who fought to change the world—
"Leap and a net will appear."*

Introduction BY ELLEN KLAGES

The James Tiptree Jr. Award

The award is given each year for a work of science fiction or fantasy that explores or expands gender roles. It was created in 1991 by Pat Murphy and Karen Joy Fowler, as a reaction to the fact that, at the time, all SF awards were named after men. Pat says that it was started as "an effort to reward writers who were pushing against gender expectations," and also to give her an interesting topic for her Guest of Honor speech at WisCon 15. WisCon, the world's only feminist-oriented SF convention, seemed like the perfect place to launch an award that "looks for work that resists narrow definitions of political correctness, and is thought-provoking, imaginative, and perhaps even infuriating." Karen, a troublemaker, but a thoughtful one, suggested it be funded by bake sales. World Domination Through Chocolate Chip Cookies! It was greeted with great enthusiasm, and the rest is history.

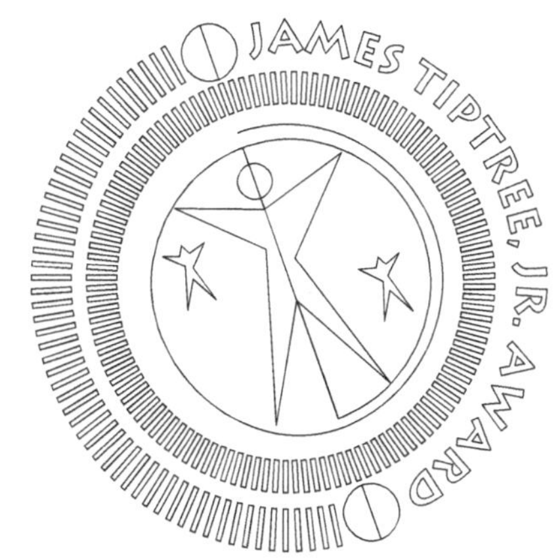

Why Tiptree?

Pat and Karen named the award for Alice Sheldon, who wrote under the pseudonym James Tiptree Jr. When Sheldon began writing in the late 1960s, she thought "a male name seemed like good camouflage." Mulling over various pen names, she saw a jar of Tiptree marmalade in the supermarket. "James Tiptree," she said. "Junior," her husband added. For the next decade, James Tiptree won every major SF award, and "his" writing was described as "ineluctably masculine." The discovery of her true identity rocked the SF field. She is most notable for breaking down the perceived barrier between "male" and "female" voices, and was inducted into the SF Hall of Fame in 2012. Her writing made her beloved; her masquerade made her a legend.

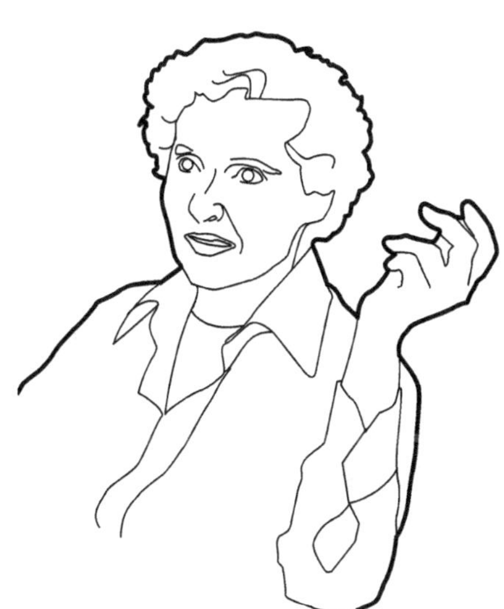

Space Babe

Space Babe first appeared in 1997 on a temporary tattoo, sold as a fundraiser for the James Tiptree Jr. Award. She was designed by Jeanne Gomoll, who adapted an image of a ray-gun wielding space pirate taken from the cover of a 1953 comic book. Space Babe quickly became the symbol of the award, and of its supporters, the Secret Feminist Cabal. For two decades, auctioneer Ellen Klages recreated popular culture as if a feminist super-hero had always existed: pages from *Cabal Comix*, WWII-era posters, 1970s animation cels, and other faux souvenirs. Now, with the images in this book, Jeanne Gomoll once again reimagines Space Babe as a symbol of the true diversity of our times. The Secret Feminist Cabal is growing every year, and our mission continues to be changing the world, and standing up for human rights for everyone, everywhere. We are all Space Babes. Won't you pick up a crayon and join us?

—Ellen Klages / March, 2018

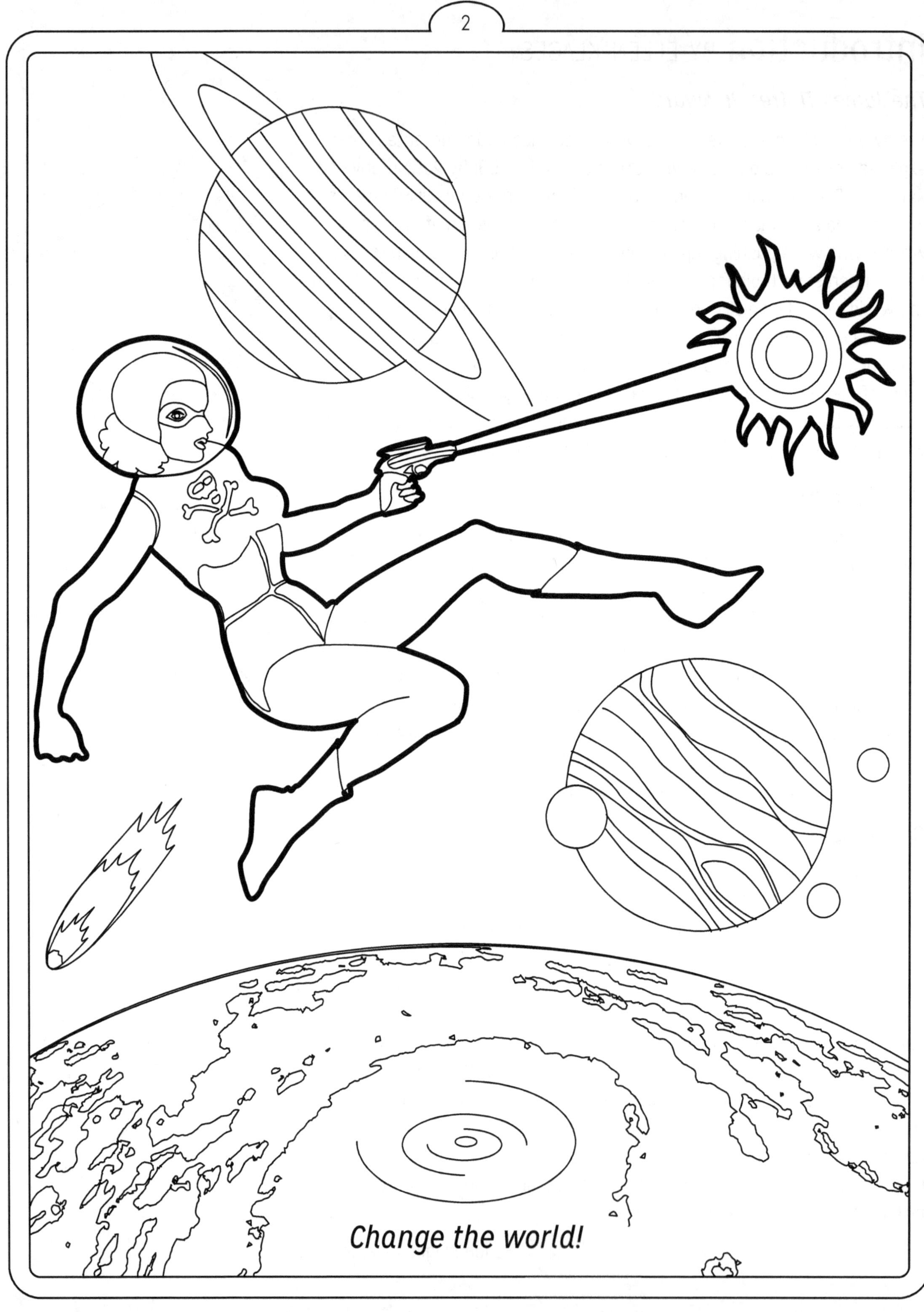
Change the world!

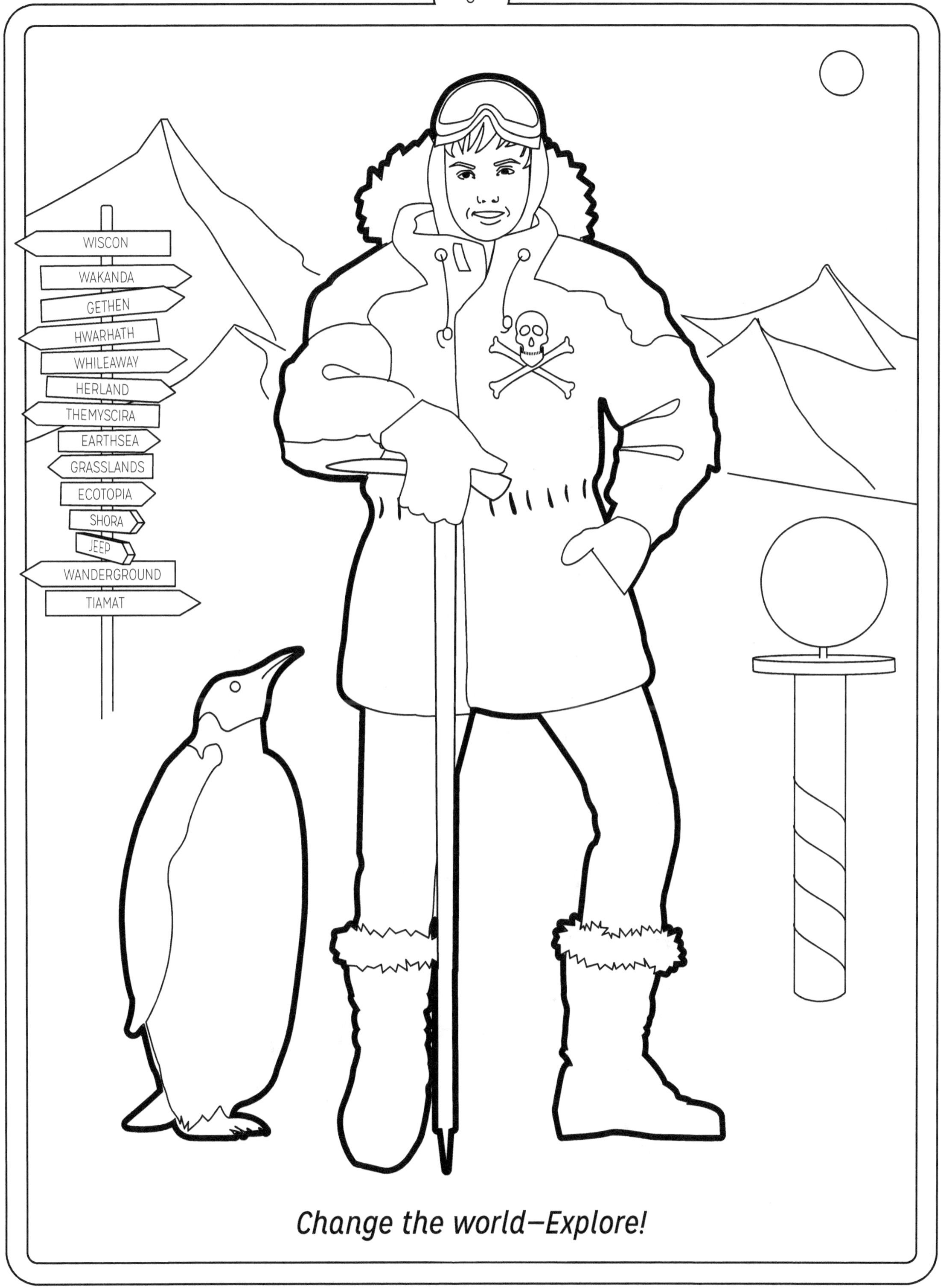

Change the world—Explore!

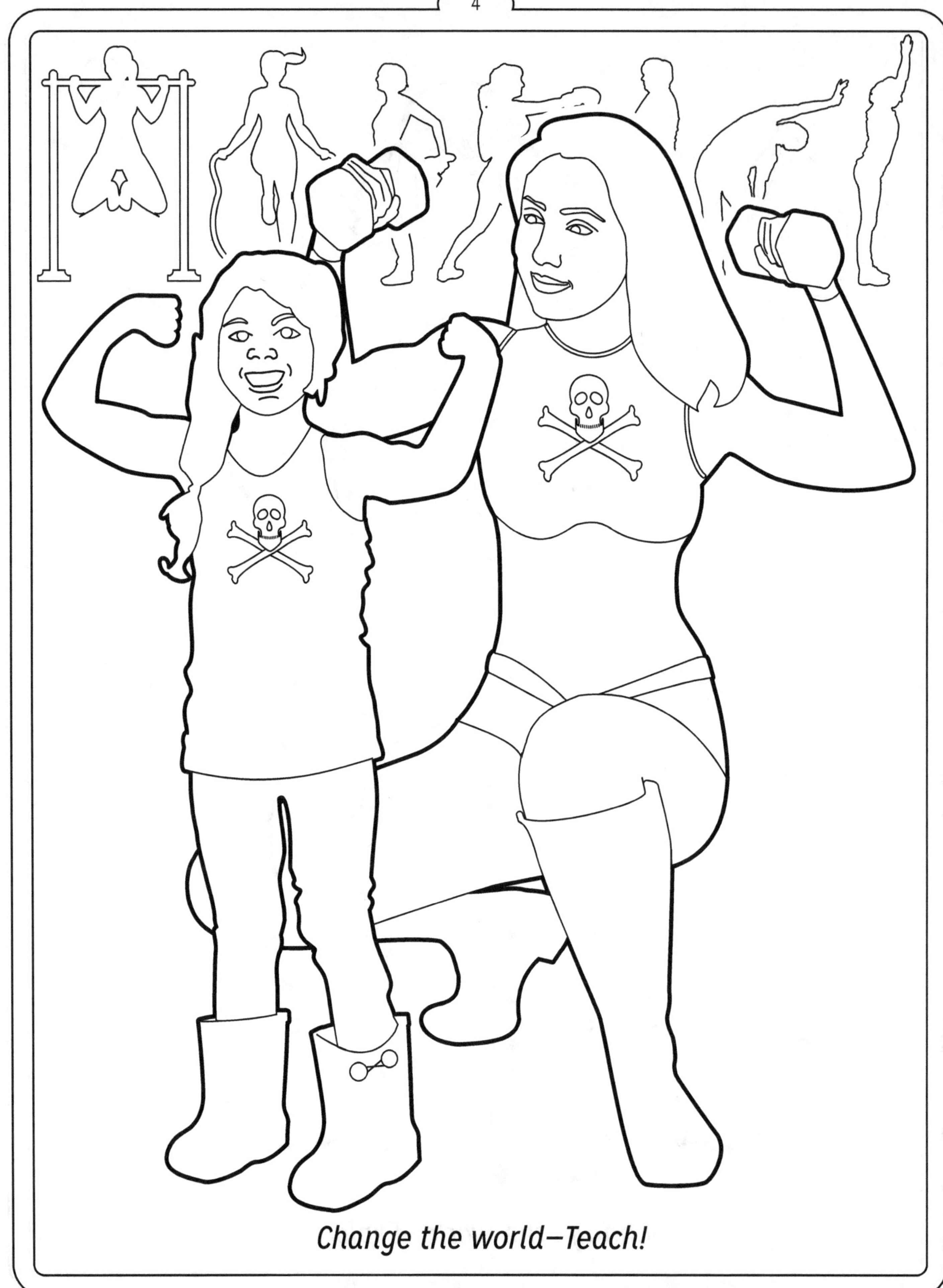

Change the world—Teach!

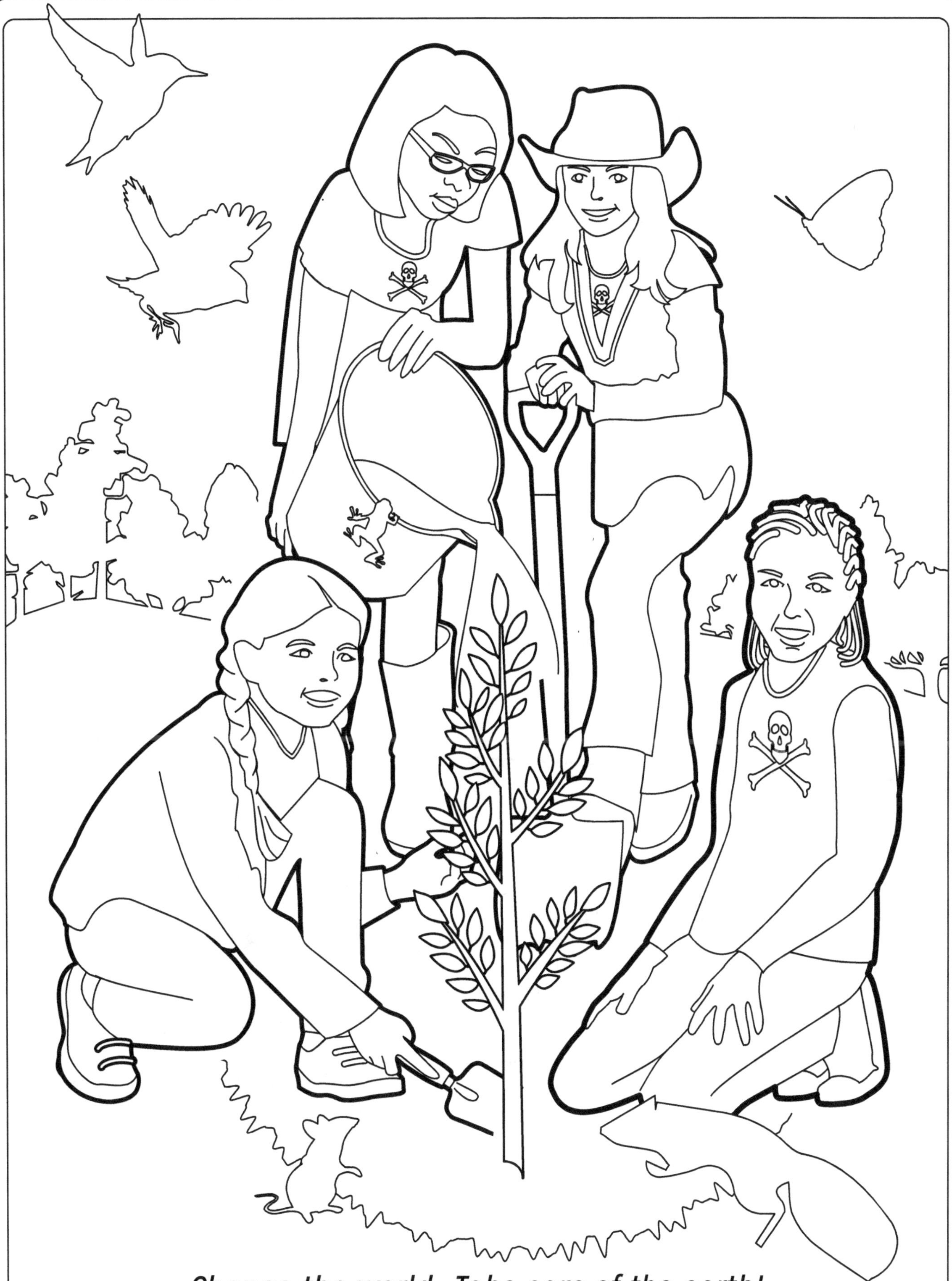

Change the world—Take care of the earth!

Camping Cookies

Space Babe's Favorite Cookies

¾ cup butter

1 cup brown sugar, firmly packed

½ cup granulated sugar

1 egg

¼ cup water

1 teaspoon vanilla

3 cups oatmeal, uncooked

1 cup flour

1 teaspoon salt

½ teaspoon baking soda

1 cup nuts, chopped

1 cup chocolate chips

1 cup coconut

½ cup dried cherries, chopped

Preheat oven to 350°F. Beat together butter, sugars, egg, water and vanilla until creamy. Combine and add remaining dry ingredients. Mix well. Add nuts, chocolate chips, coconut and cherries. Drop by rounded teaspoonfuls onto greased cookie sheet. Bake at 350°F for 12–15 minutes.

The James Tiptree Jr. Award Bake Sale

The James Tiptree Jr. Award sponsors bake sales at WisCon and other conventions, for which Tiptree supporters bake delicious goodies. Other supporters, and sometimes the same ones, buy and enjoy those baked goodies, content in the knowledge that the calories are consumed for a good cause!

https://tiptree.org/support-us/host-a-bakesale

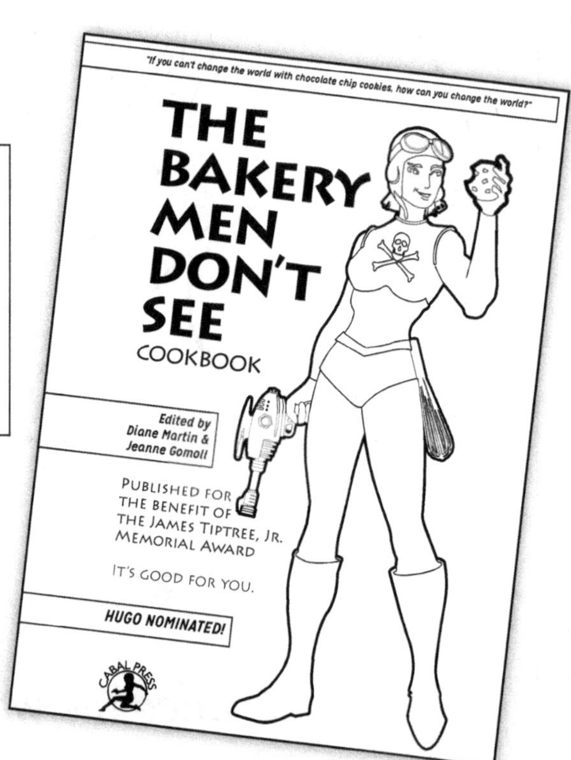

Space Babe appears on the cover of the revised version of the cookbook, *The Bakery Men Don't See.*

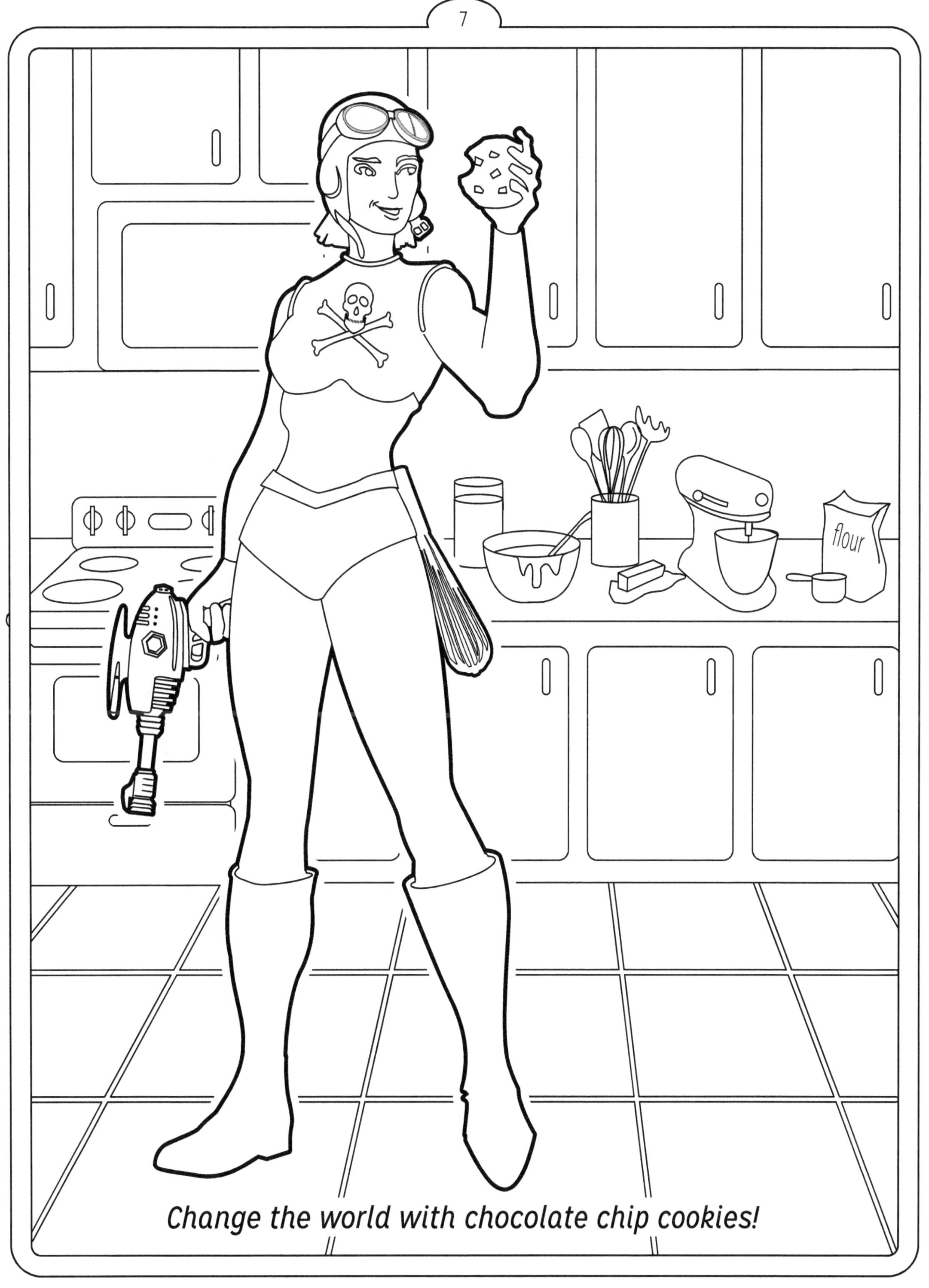

Change the world with chocolate chip cookies!

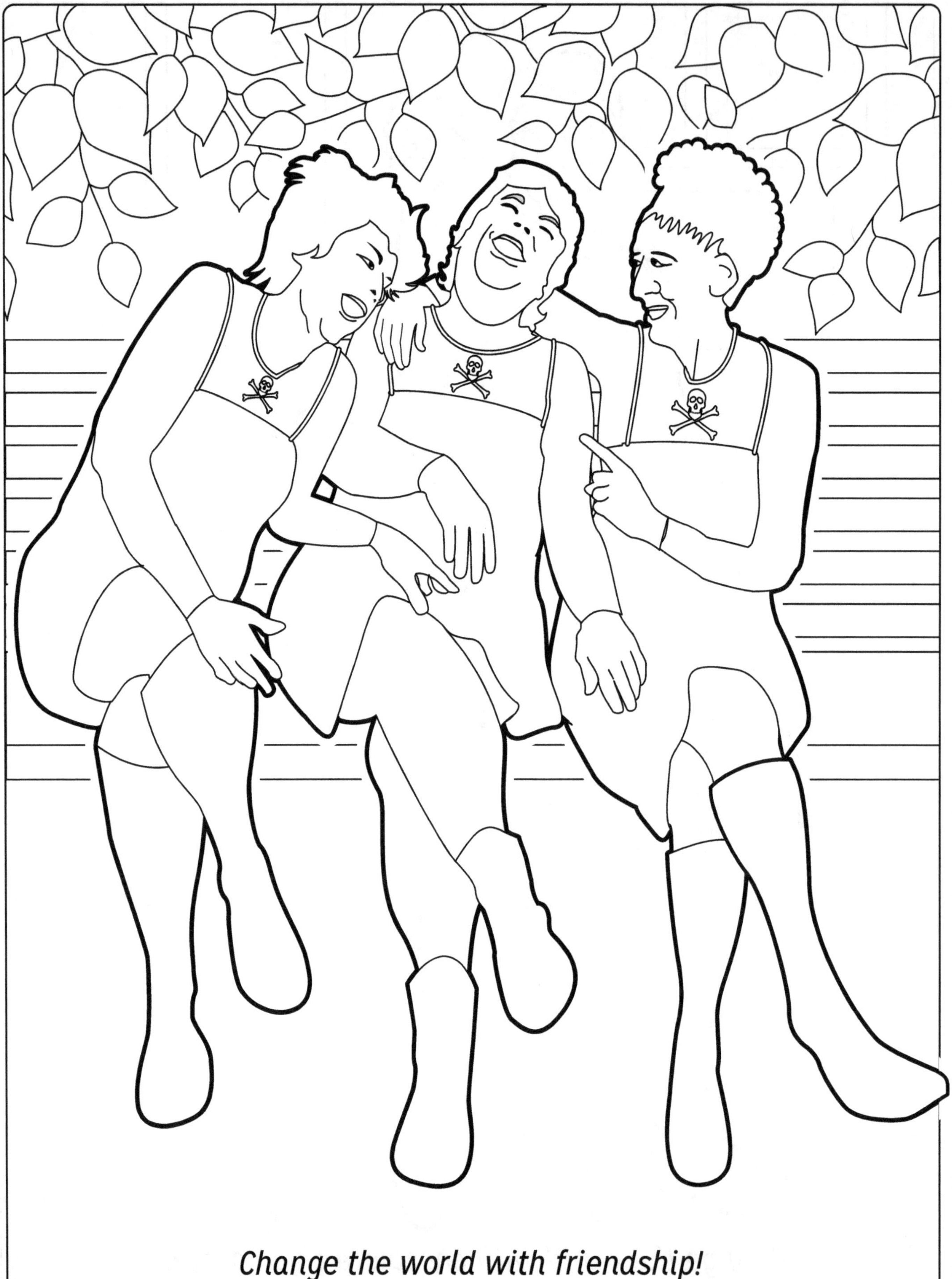

Change the world with friendship!

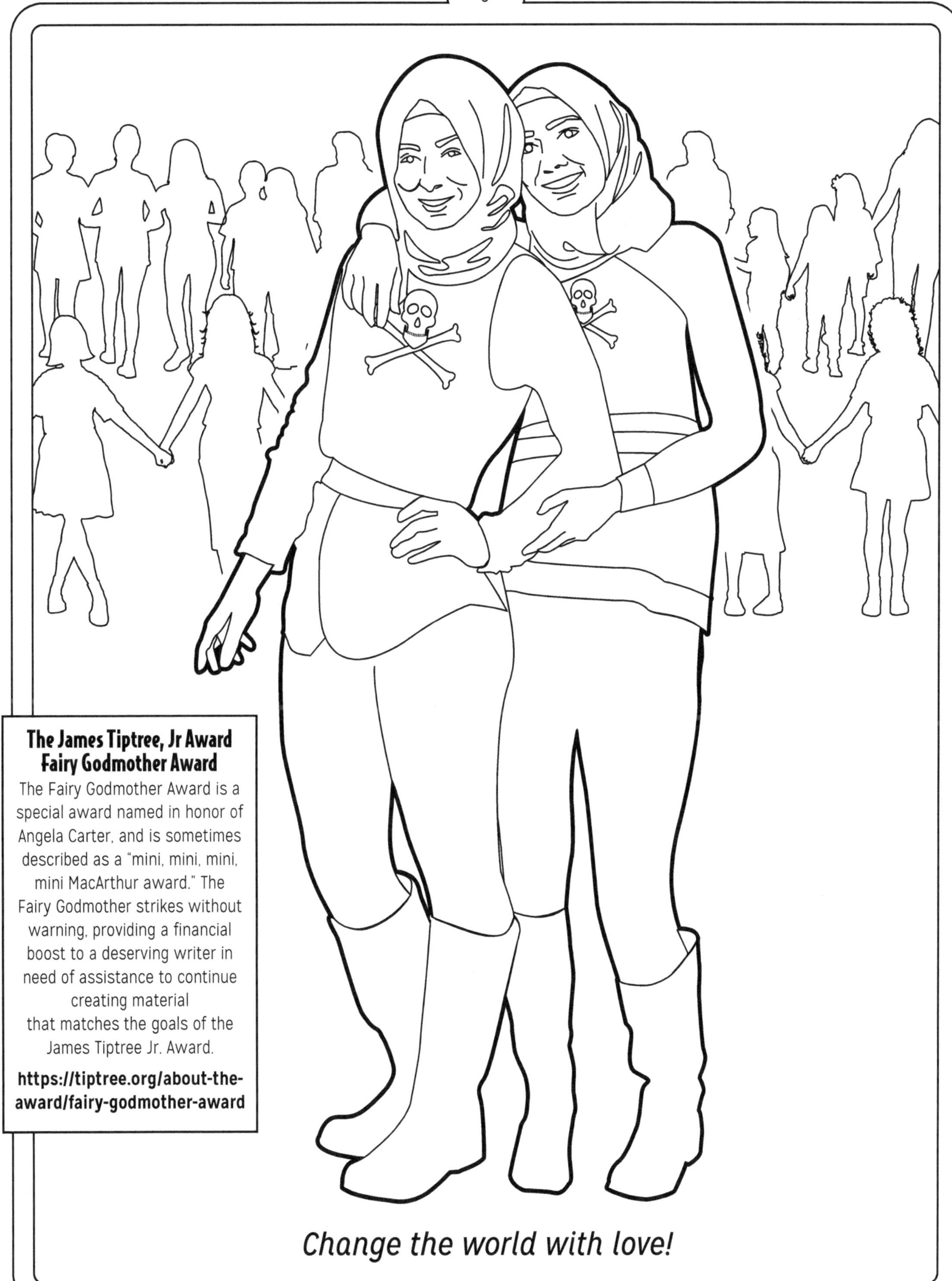

The James Tiptree, Jr Award
Fairy Godmother Award

The Fairy Godmother Award is a special award named in honor of Angela Carter, and is sometimes described as a “mini, mini, mini, mini MacArthur award.” The Fairy Godmother strikes without warning, providing a financial boost to a deserving writer in need of assistance to continue creating material that matches the goals of the James Tiptree Jr. Award.

https://tiptree.org/about-the-award/fairy-godmother-award

Change the world with love!

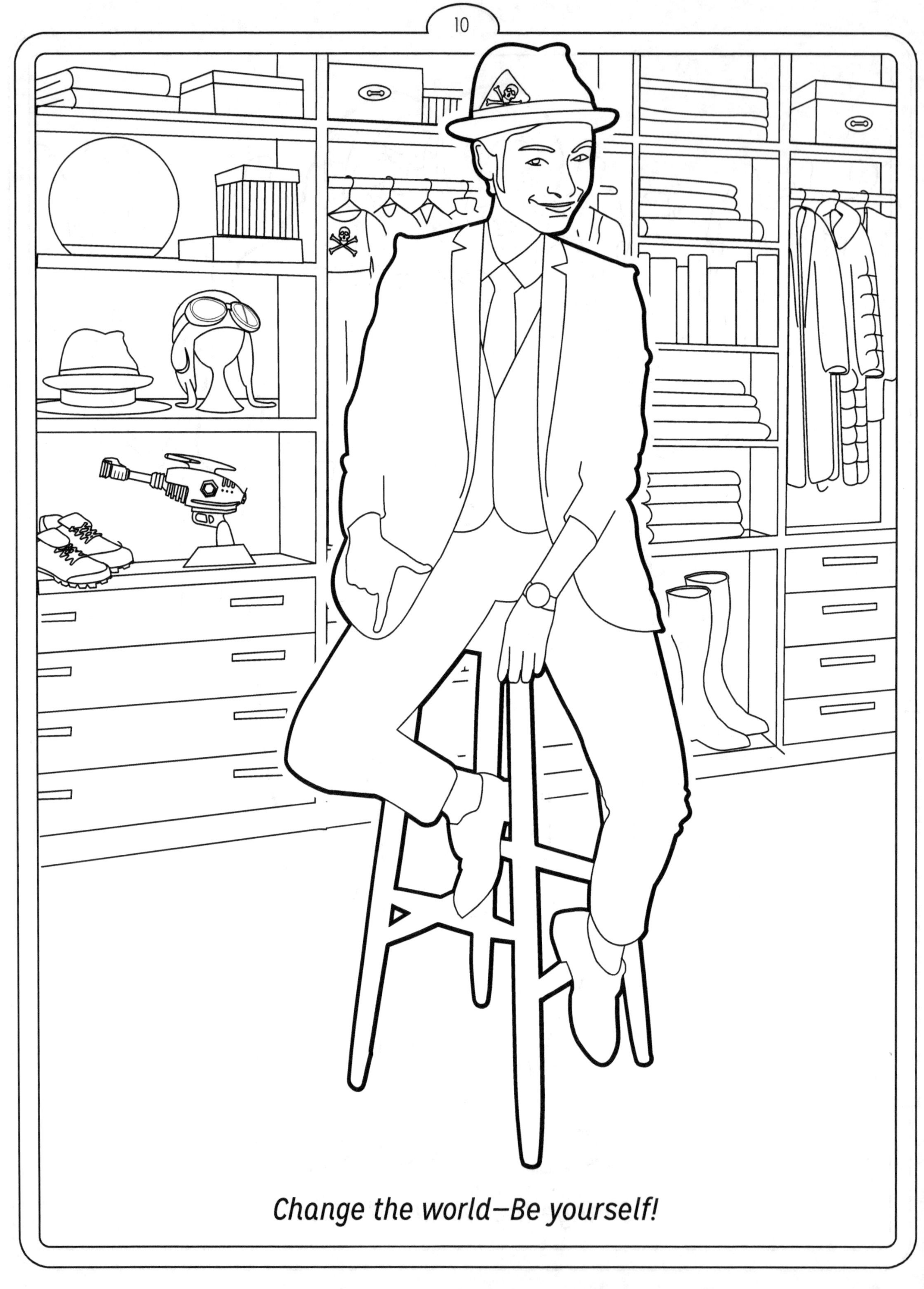

Change the world—Be yourself!

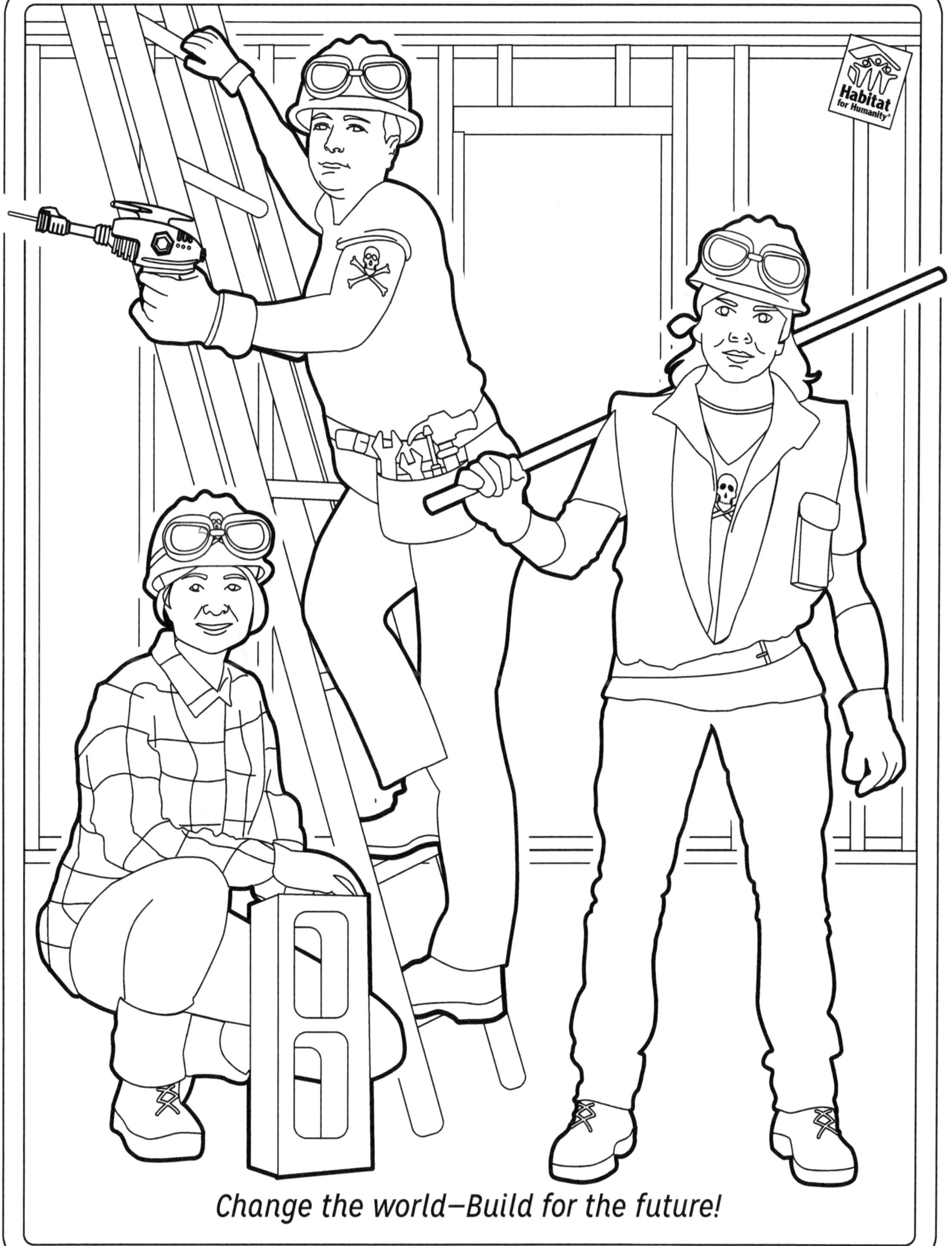

Change the world—Build for the future!

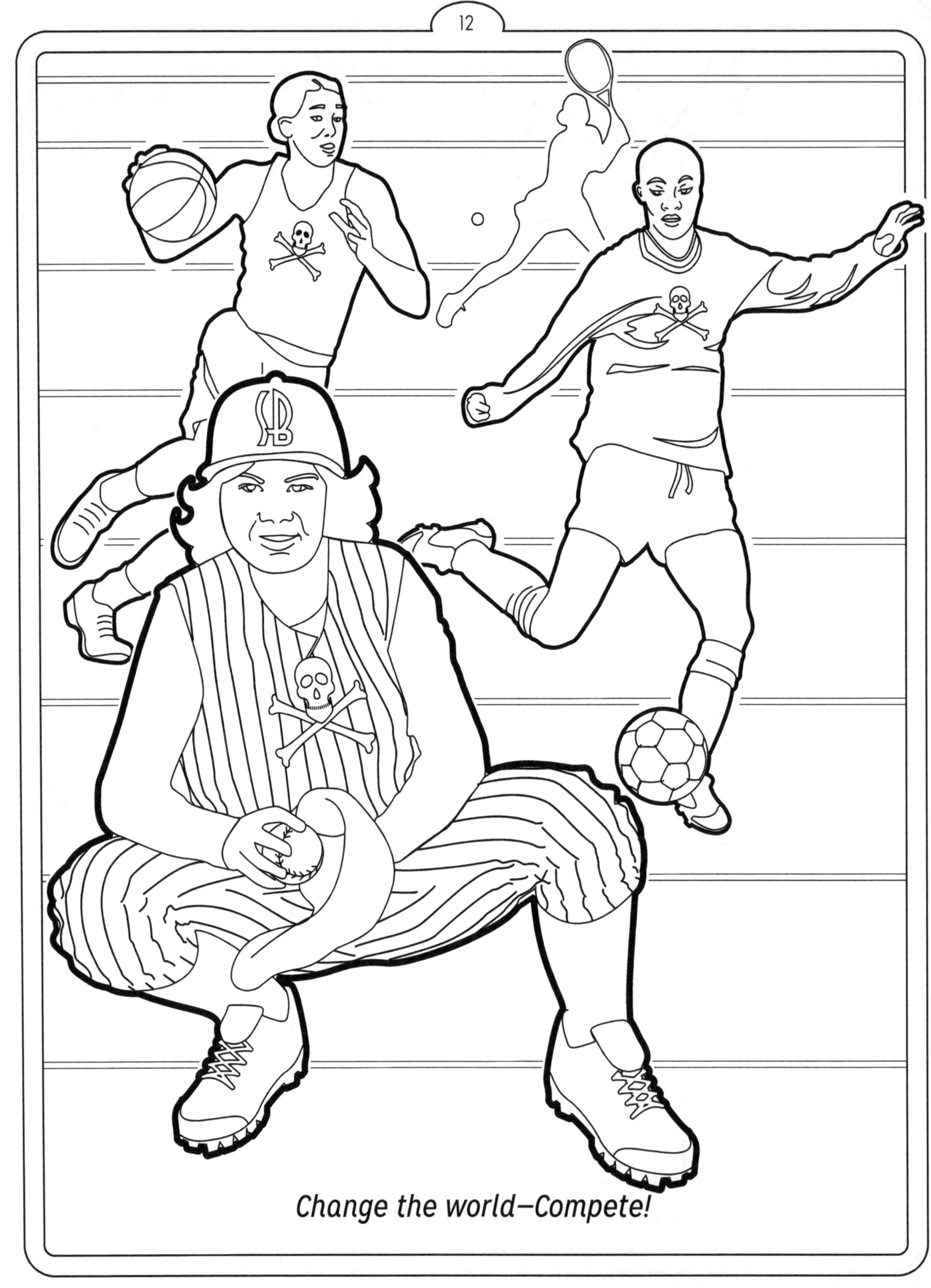

Change the world—Compete!

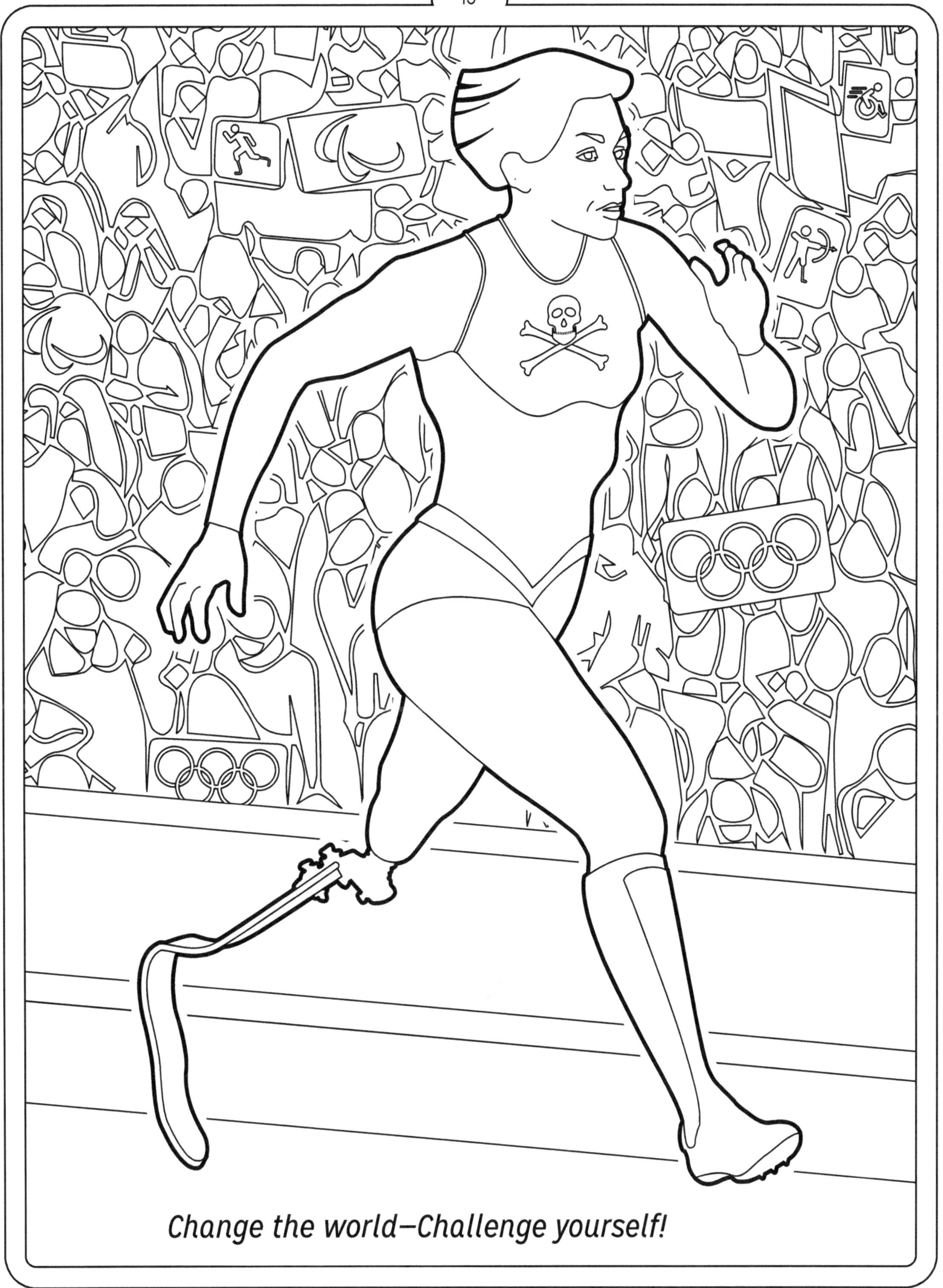

Change the world—Challenge yourself!

A

B

Make your own

Intergalactic Space Babe Tiara

1) Photocopy pages 14 and 15.
2) Color your tiara and headband!
3) Glue the colored copies onto heavy (but bendable) paper.
4) Cut out the 3 pieces from the mounted copies – both the tiara front piece and the 2-part headband.
5) Tape the head bands to the tiara front – Attach A to A and B to B.
6) Size the tiara's headband to your head and tape to fit.

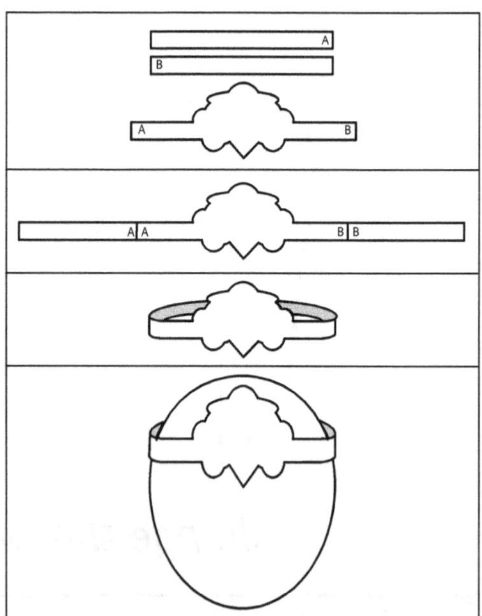

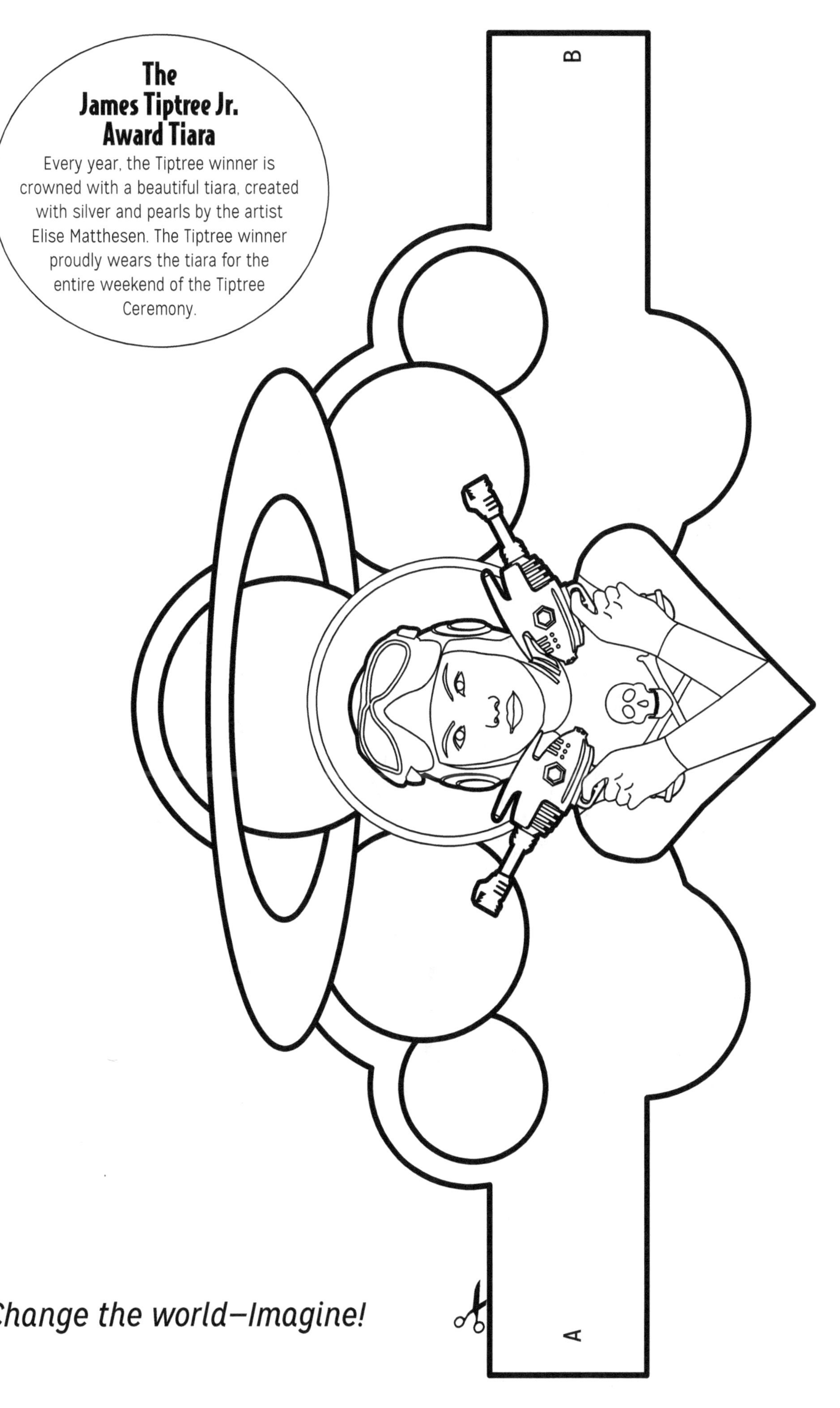

The James Tiptree Jr. Award Tiara

Every year, the Tiptree winner is crowned with a beautiful tiara, created with silver and pearls by the artist Elise Matthesen. The Tiptree winner proudly wears the tiara for the entire weekend of the Tiptree Ceremony.

Change the world—Imagine!

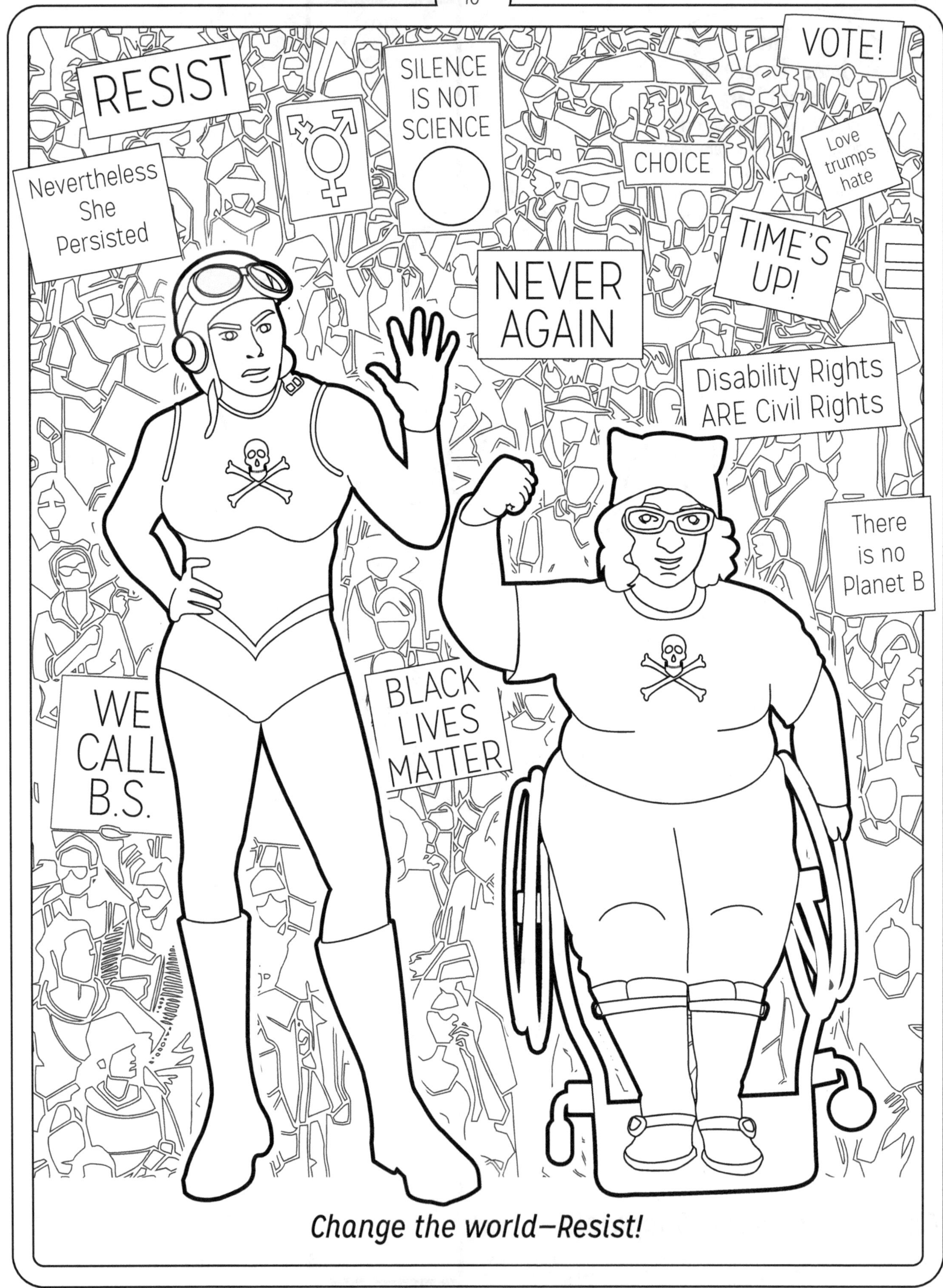

Change the world—Resist!

Shirley Chisholm
1924–2005. First woman to run for president of the United States, in 1972.

Sojourner Truth 1797–1883. An abolitionist and women's rights activist.

Susan B. Anthony
1820–1906. Fought for a constitutional amendment giving women the right to vote.

Elizabeth Cady Stanton
1815–1902. Convened the famous Seneca Falls Convention in July 1848, and took the lead in proposing laws to grant women the right to vote.

Hilary Clinton 1947–. Ran for president of the United States in 2008 and 2016.

Who will be the first woman president of the United States?

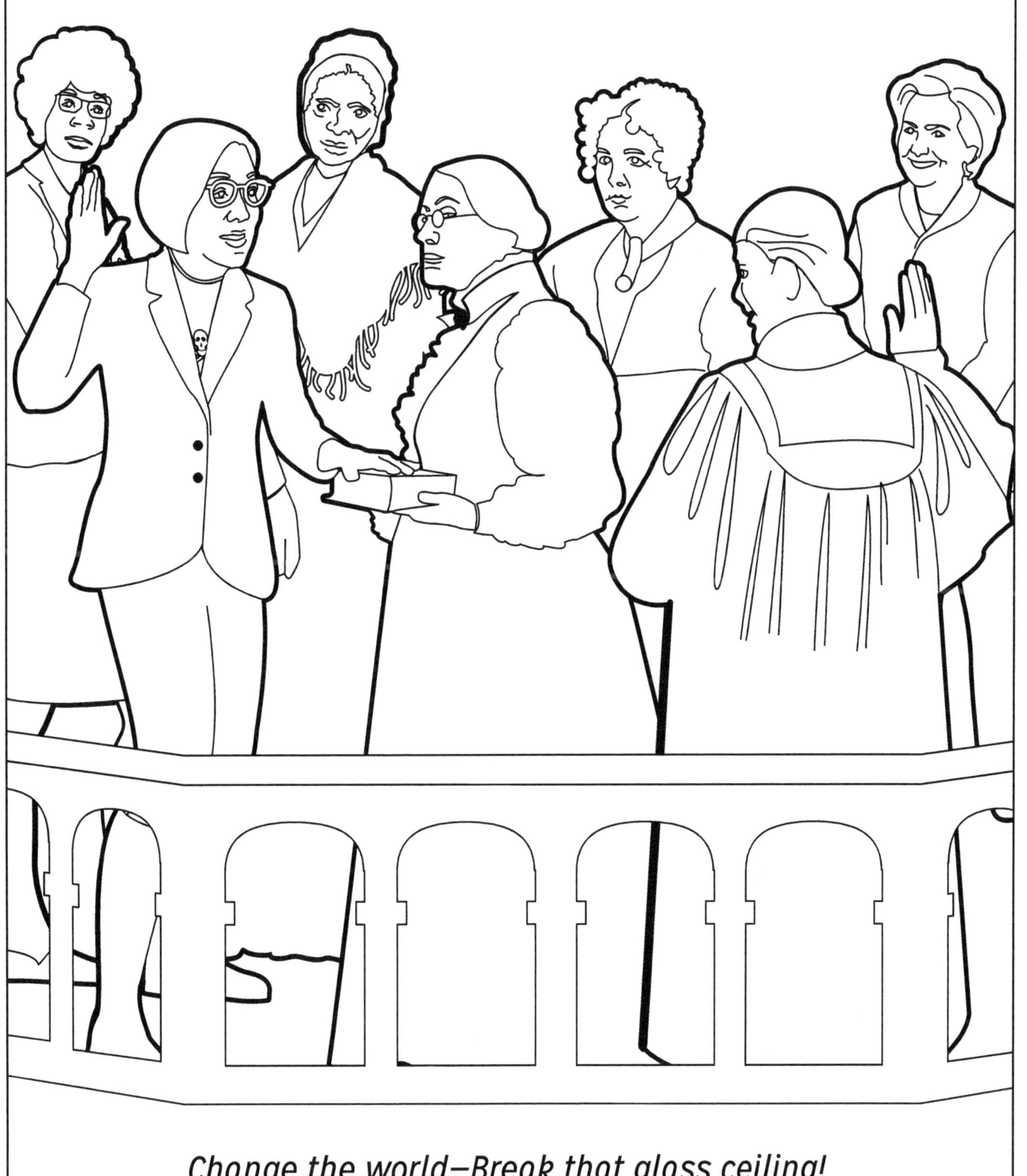

Change the world—Break that glass ceiling!

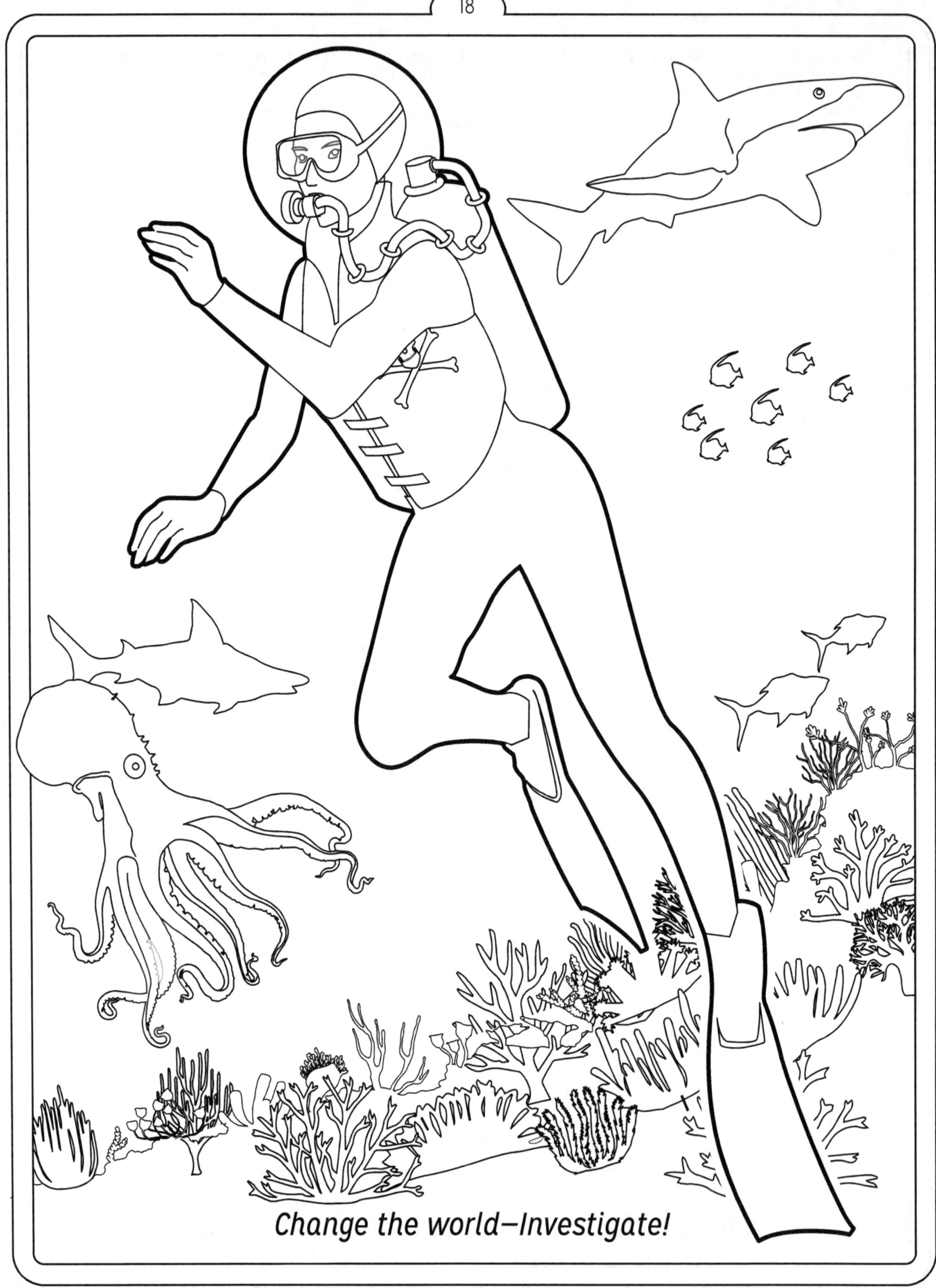

Change the world—Investigate!

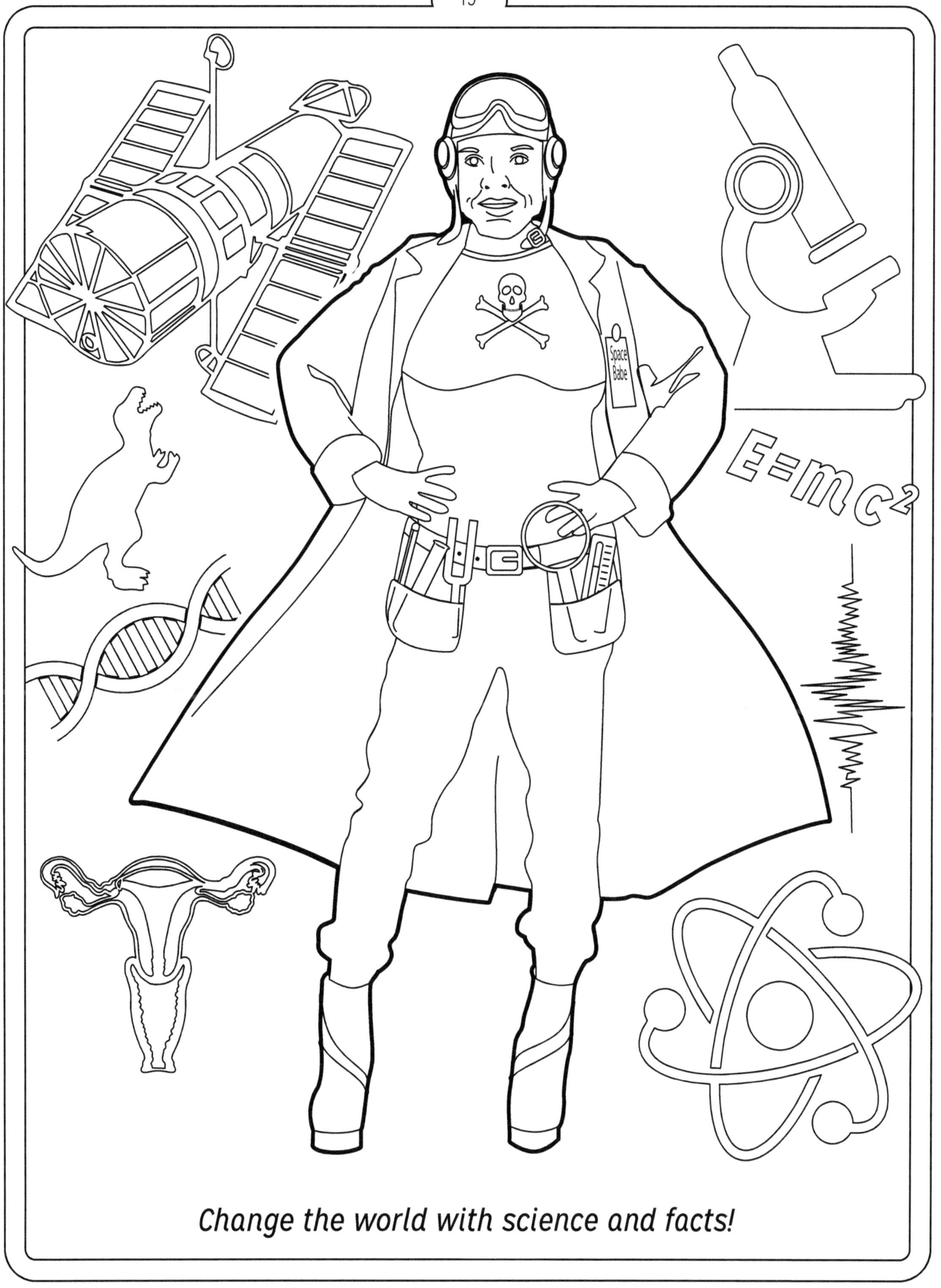

Change the world with science and facts!

Ursula K. Le Guin, 1929–2018
The most celebrated author in James Tiptree Jr. Award history.
She was a friend to Space Babe.

Ursula K. Le Guin won the James Tiptree Jr. Award 2 times.

"The Matter of Seggri"
in Crank! #3, Broken Mirrors Press, 1994

"Mountain Ways"
Asimov's Science Fiction, August 1996

Ursula K. Le Guin was celebrated on the Tiptree Honor List 4 times.

"Forgiveness Day"
Asimov's Science Fiction, November 1994

A Fisherman of the Inland Sea
Harper, 1994

"Unchosen Love"
in *More Amazing Stories*, edited by Kim Mohan, Tor Books, 1998

Lavinia
Harcourt, 2008

Ursula K. Le Guin was featured on 3 Tiptree Long Lists.

"Dragonfly"
in *Legends: Short Novels by the Masters of Modern Fantasy*,
edited by Robert Silverberg; Tor Books, 1998

"Wild Girls"
Asimov's Science Fiction, March 2002

"Seasons of the Ansarac"
Infinite Matrix, June 3 2002

Ursula K. Le Guin was honored with a Retrospective James Tiptree Jr. Award.

The Left Hand of Darkness
1969

Ursula K. Le Guin served 2 times as a judge for the James Tiptree Jr. Award.

1993 and 2004

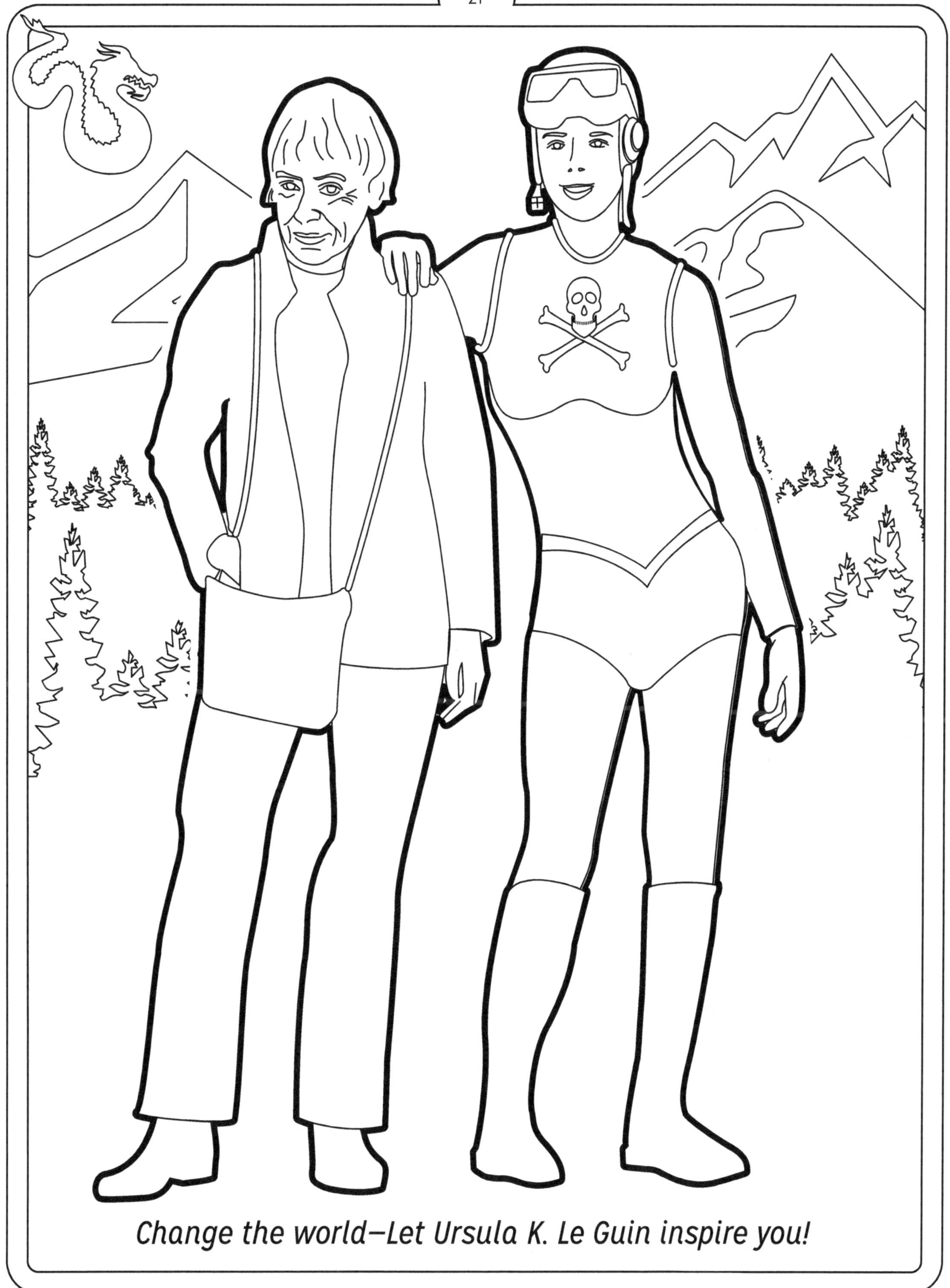

Change the world—Let Ursula K. Le Guin inspire you!

Winner of the 2017 James Tiptree Jr. Award

Who Runs the World?, by Virginia Bergin

(Macmillan Children's Books, UK, 2017)
US Title: *The XY* (Sourcebooks, US, 2018)

For more information about the 2017 winner, Honor list and Long List, visit **www.tiptree.org**

2017 James Tiptree Jr. Award Honor List

"Don't Press Charges and I Won't Sue,"
by Charlie Jane Anders
Boston Review, 2017

The Devourers, by Indra Das
Del Rey, 2016

Dreadnought and *Sovereign*,
by April Daniels
Diversion, 2017

An Excess Male, by Maggie Shen King
Harper Voyager, 2017

Her Body and Other Parties,
by Carmen Maria Machado
Gray Wolf, 2017

An Unkindness of Ghosts,
by Rivers Solomon
Akashic, 2017

"Black Tides of Heaven" and
"Red Threads of Fortune,"
by JY Yang
Tor, 2017

2017 James Tiptree Jr. Award Long List

The Power, Naomi Alderman (Viking, UK, 2016)

"Palingenesis," Megan Arkenberg (*Shimmer*, 2016)

Conspiracy of Ravens, Lila Bowen (Orbit, 2016)

O Human Star, vol. 1 and 2, Blue Dellaquanti (self published, 2017)

The Strange Case of the Alchemist's Daughter, Theodora Goss (Saga, 2017)

The Book of Etta, Meg Elison (47 North, 2017)

"Notes from Liminal Spaces," Hiromi Goto (*Uncanny Magazine*, 2017)

"The Little Homo Sapiens Scientist", SL Huang (*Book Smugglers*, 2016)

"Your Body, by Default," Alexis A. Hunter (*Fireside Magazine*, 2016)

The Stars Are Legion, Kameron Hurley (Saga, 2017)

The Moon and the Other, John Kessel (Saga, 2017)

Passing Strange, Ellen Klages (Tor, 2017)

Monstress, Volumes 1 and 2, Marjorie Liu and Sana Takeda (Image, 2016)

"Coral Bones," Foz Meadows (*Monstrous Little Voices*, Rebellion, UK, 2016)

Provenance, Ann Leckie (Orbit, 2017)

"Her Sacred Spirit Soars," S. Qiouyi Li (*Strange Horizons*, 2016)

The Art of Starving, Sam J. Miller (Harper, 2017)

Infect Your Friends and Loved Ones, Torrey Peters (self published, 2016)

Autonomous, Annalee Newitz (Tor, 2017)

Magnus Chase and the Hammer of Thor, Rick Riordan (Hyperion, 2017)

The Tiger's Daughter, K. Arsenault Rivera (Tor, 2017)

Viscera, Gabby Squailia (published as Gabriel Squalia, Talos, 2016)

"Small Changes Over Long Periods of Time," K.M. Szpara (*Uncanny*, 2017)

Known Associates, thingswithwings (self published at *Archive of Our Own*, USA, 2016)

Story sequence by Debbie Urbanski:

"The Portal," (*The Sun*, 2016)

"The Thread," (*Cicada*, 2016)

"A List of My Utopias," (*The Sun*, 2017)

"How to Find a Portal," (*Lightspeed*, 2017)

"A Few Personal Observations About Portals," (*The Sun*, 2017)

"A Fist of Permutations in Lightning and Wildflowers," Alyssa Wong (Tor.com, 2016)

Change the world—Send your suggestions for the 2018 James Tiptree Jr. Award to the Tiptree judges! **https://tiptree.org**

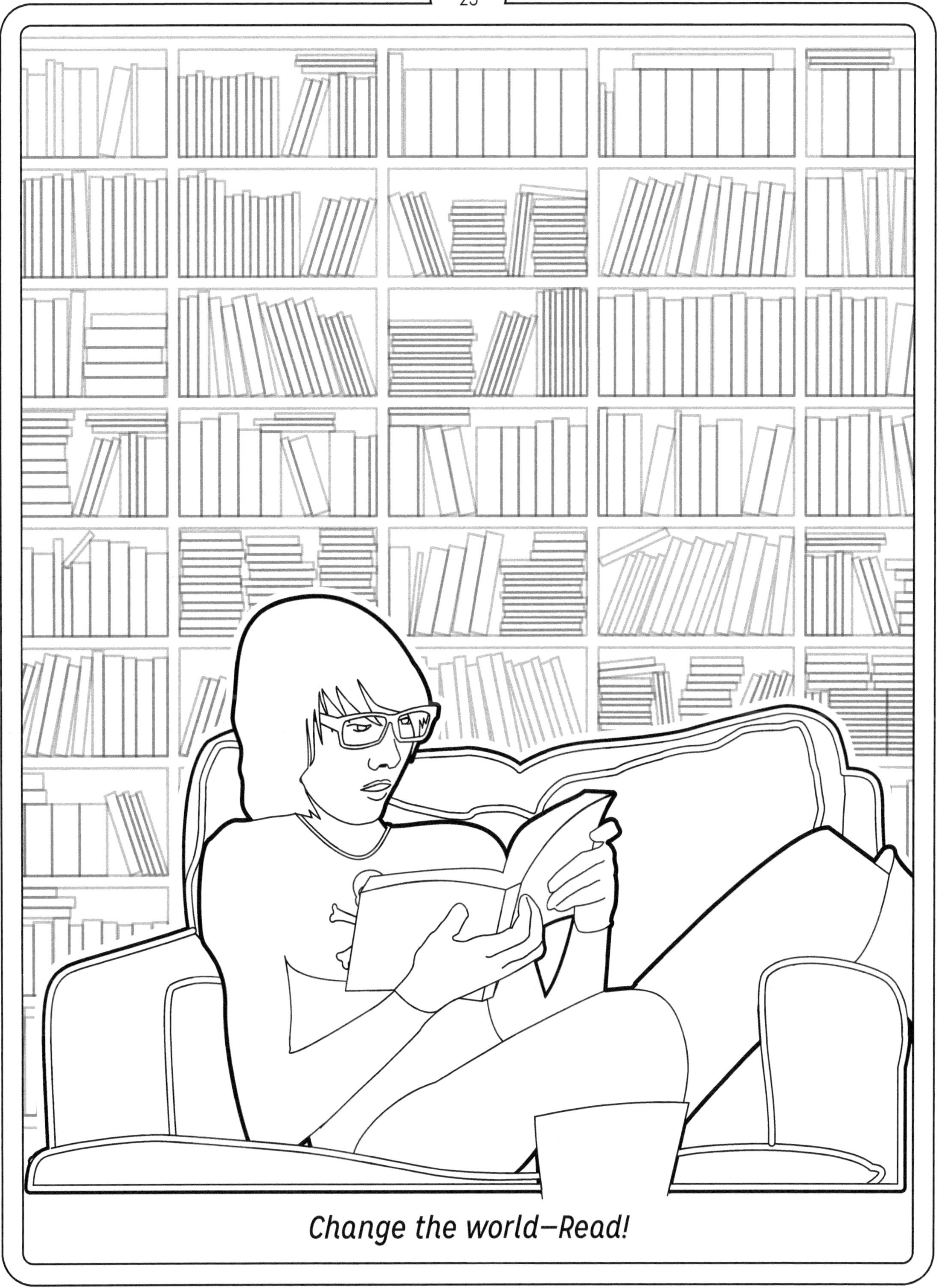

Change the world—Read!

Write your own Space Babe adventure!

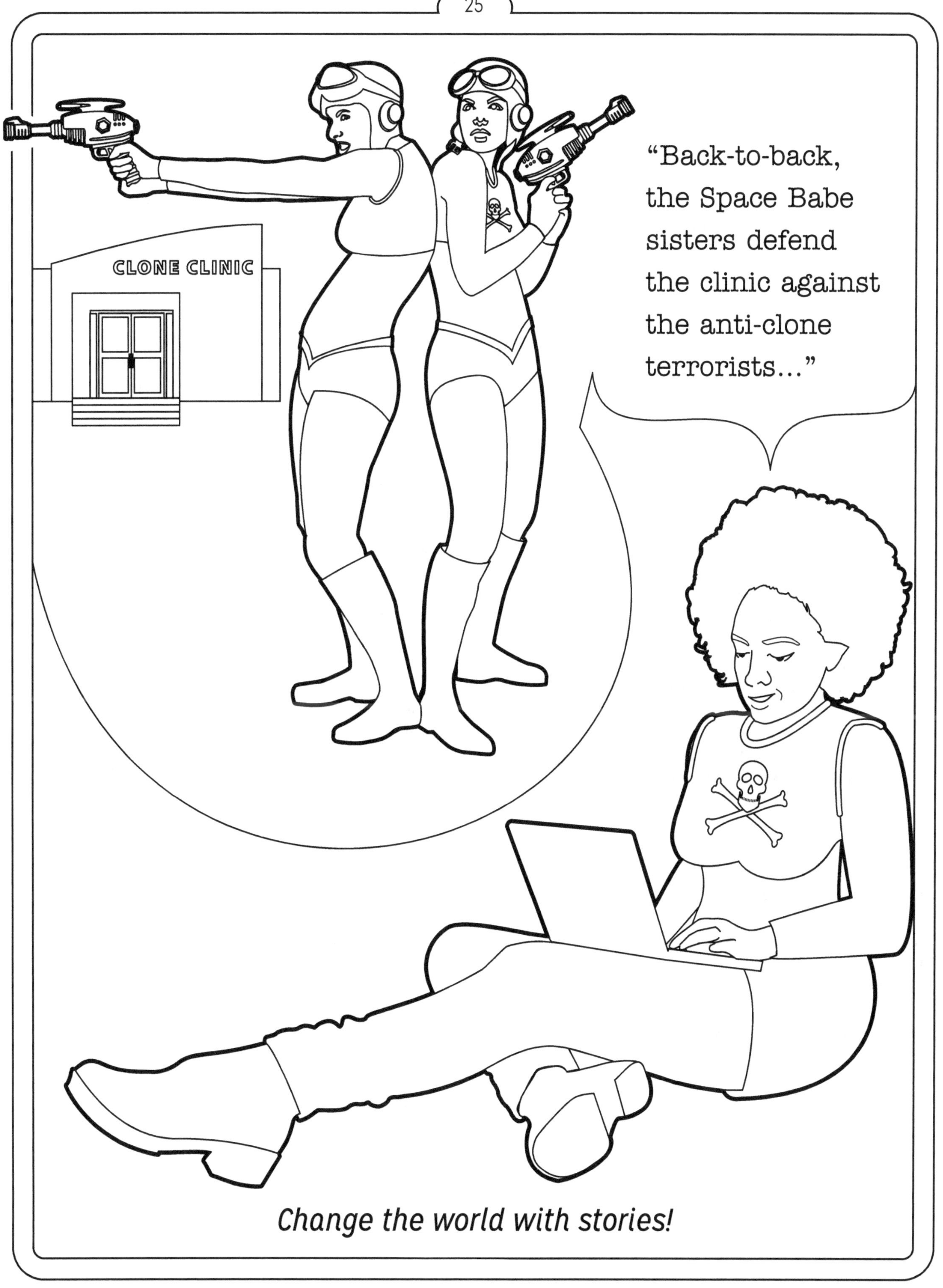

Change the world with stories!

Space Babe Song

by F. J. Bergmann

She considers all the options; she wants to be a world-changer.
When others need her she won't hesitate to put herself in danger.
She seeks out every challenge: an interplanetary ranger,
She's a Space Babe, Space Babe, Space Babe!
[repeat after each stanza]

Through geography and spacetime, she's an intrepid explorer.
She won't ignore the world nor allow others to deplore her,
These journeys of discovery are delights that will restore her.

Today she's a small bud, but tomorrow she will flower,
She'll work out hard and grow up, hour after hour.
Space Babe can be her teacher so she'll find her superpower!

A responsible Terran, she cares for air and water
And the land that we live on, just like she oughta.
The universe's baby, she's our mother Earth's daughter.

No revolution can succeed without a good cook and baker.
No invention can succeed without a dedicated maker.
Nobody ends up woke without a Space Babe to wake her.

She reaches out to everyone with friendship and lovin'—
And anyone who listens is welcome in her coven
Where there's tea in the kettle and cookies in the oven.

A Space Babe reaches out with kindness to others as a lover.
No matter how she's been hurt, with help she can recover.
She's a heroine we idolize, and that's why we love her.

A Space Babe of any gender can dress up to be dapper
And promenade in public, as chill as any rapper.
Space Babe learns from history, but won't let the past trap her.

She's building up, not tearing down: Space Babe is a fixer.
She's constructive running meetings—or a cement mixer.
Cooperating with co-workers is a magical elixir.

Out in the field of dreams she's her own dream-catcher;
Wherever she comes from, some phoenix must have hatched her.
In outer space or inner worlds, we all want to match her.

To be an athlete doesn't need the body of a racer;
Abilities being different won't allow them to erase her.
She excels in low-gee, where she's a babe of a spacer!

She expands her mind out as far as her imagination;
Lets no one say her wildest dreams are just hallucination,
Because dreaming and ideas are the foundations of our nation.

To stand against oppression, she draws an arrow from her quiver.
She'll never let you down, never sell you up the river.
When resistance is called for, she's one who can deliver.

She fought for women's rights along with other resisters;
She marched and demonstrated despite tear gas and blisters,
And now she's changing the world for herself and her sisters.

She tries new hobbies on for size; she's learning to scuba.
If she meets a barracuda, she'll just zippity doo-dah
And focus on another skill—like playing the tuba!

Space Babe studies STEM; she truly values learning.
The sciences delight her; they're for what she's been yearning.
The fire she brings to knowledge was once a small candle burning.

She showed us what it means to be alien and human,
A true Space Babe who fantasy and sf did illumine.
Ursula K. Le Guin is our Little Bear Woman!

She can fly out past Mars just by being a reader.
If you want to win a Tiptree, well, then you'd better heed her.
With her nose in a book, she'll become tomorrow's leader.

She can weave a tale of wonder, tell a child's bedtime story.
As she learns to be a writer she will never be sorry,
Whether writing for herself, or for publishing and glory!

On any instrument she loves what notes can bring her,
and screams out all her joy in her own band as a singer.
Her song rises up as she feels the music ring her.

Anyone can be a writer, and anyone an artist.
When she draws or lifts a brush, her fingers touch stardust.
She makes wonderful worlds, and all of them are star-kissed.

You can help others whether you're a learner or a teacher.
Don't let anyone tell you that you're an overreacher;
If you want to find yourself, then join us as a seeker.
You are Space Babe, Space Babe, Space Babe!

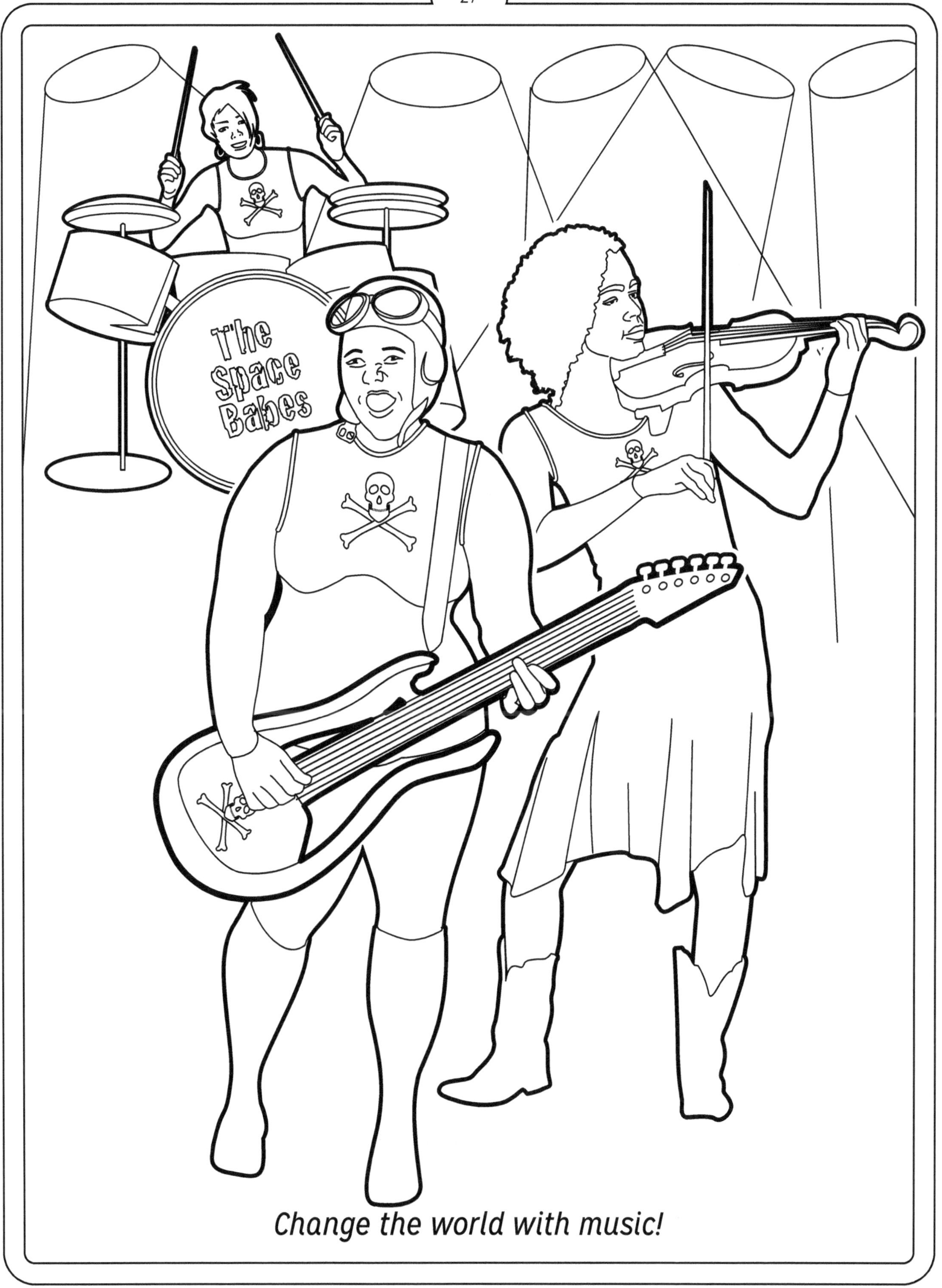

Change the world with music!

Draw yourself as Space Babe!

The James Tiptree Jr. Fellowship Award

The James Tiptree Jr. Fellowship Award celebrates writers, artists, scholars, media makers, remix artists, performers, musicians, and others. If you are doing work that is changing the way we think about gender through speculative narrative—maybe in a form we would recognize as the science fiction or fantasy genre, maybe in some other way—you are eligible for a Fellowship.

https://tiptree.org/tiptree-fellowships

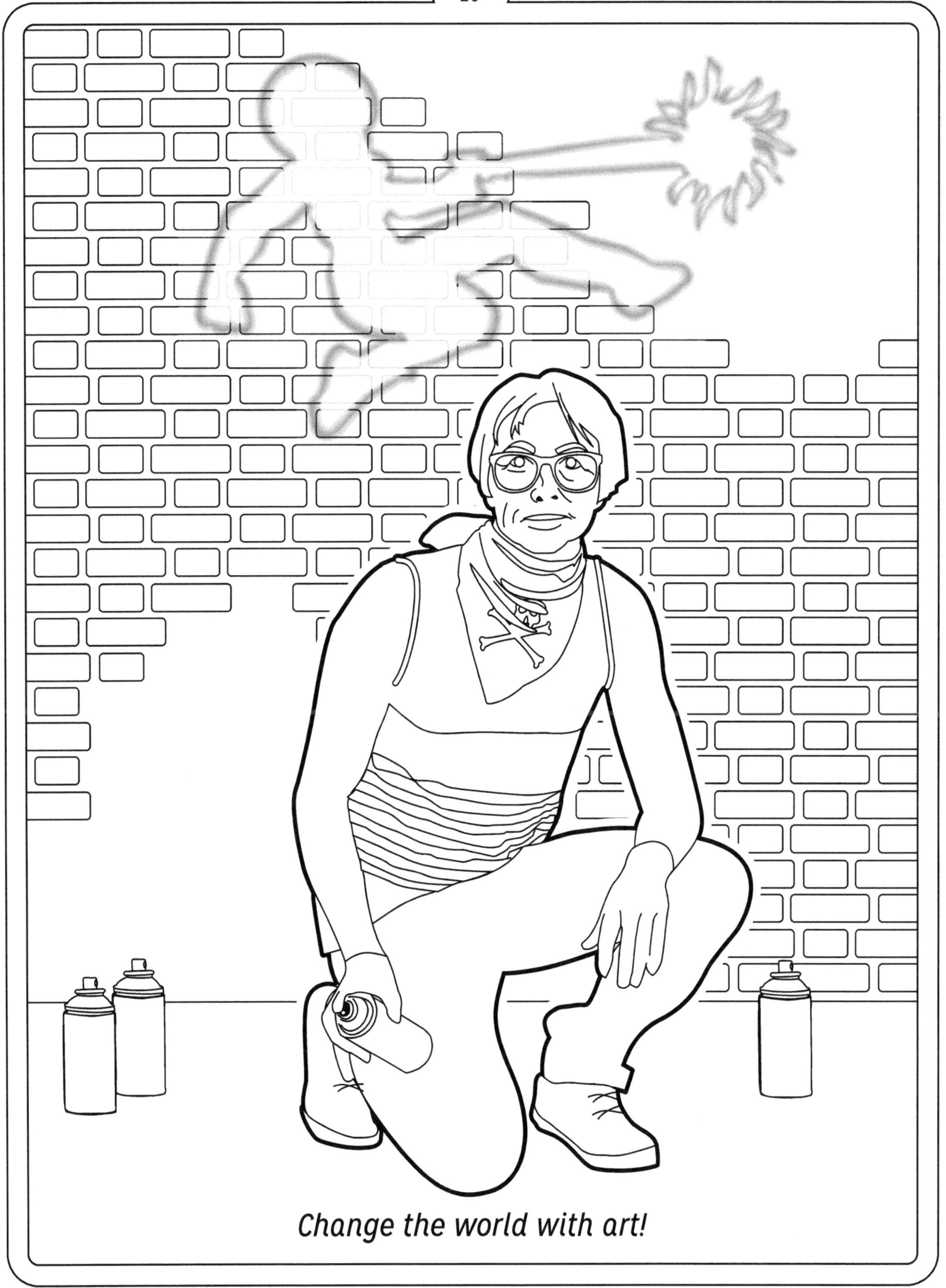

Change the world with art!

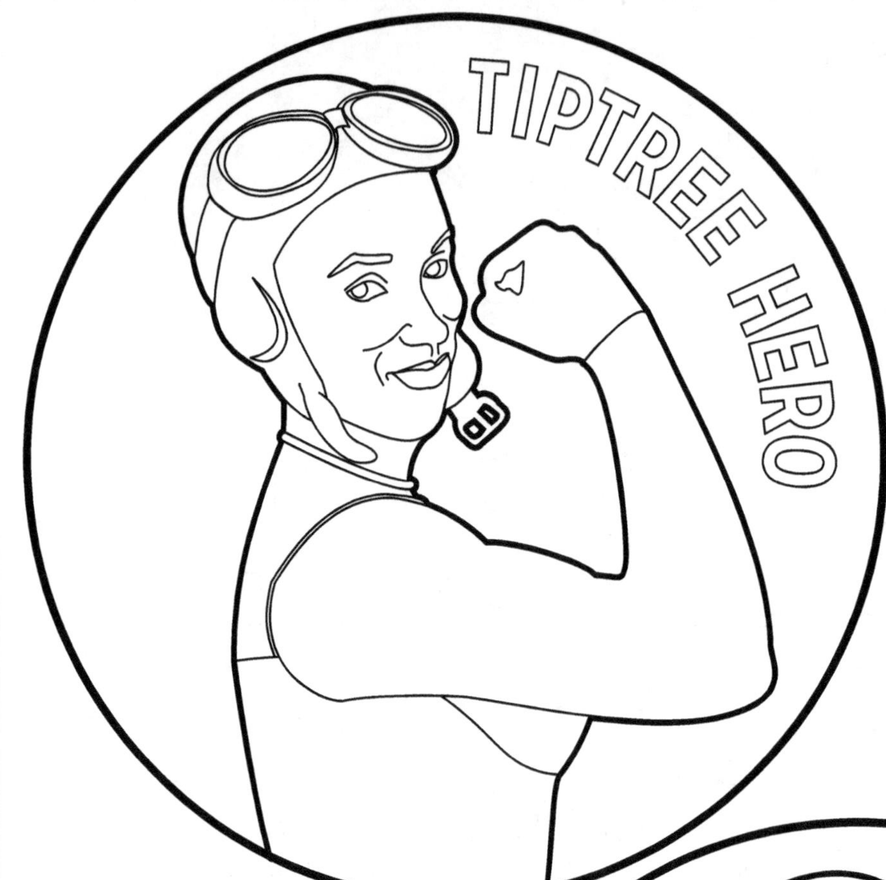

Join the Space Babe team!

1) Recommend stories and novels for the Tiptree Award at **tiptree.org**
2) Read Tiptree-Award-winning fiction and discuss with your friends.
3) Attend Tiptree Award ceremonies and serenade the winners, along with other Tiptree supporters.
4) Attend Tiptree auctions and Tiptree bakesales. Your purchases pay the cash prizes awarded to Tiptree Award winners.
5) Donate funds to support the Tiptree Award.

Here's how to earn your own Space Babe pin:

1) Bake something for a Tiptree Bake Sale.
2) Volunteer at a Tiptree auction.

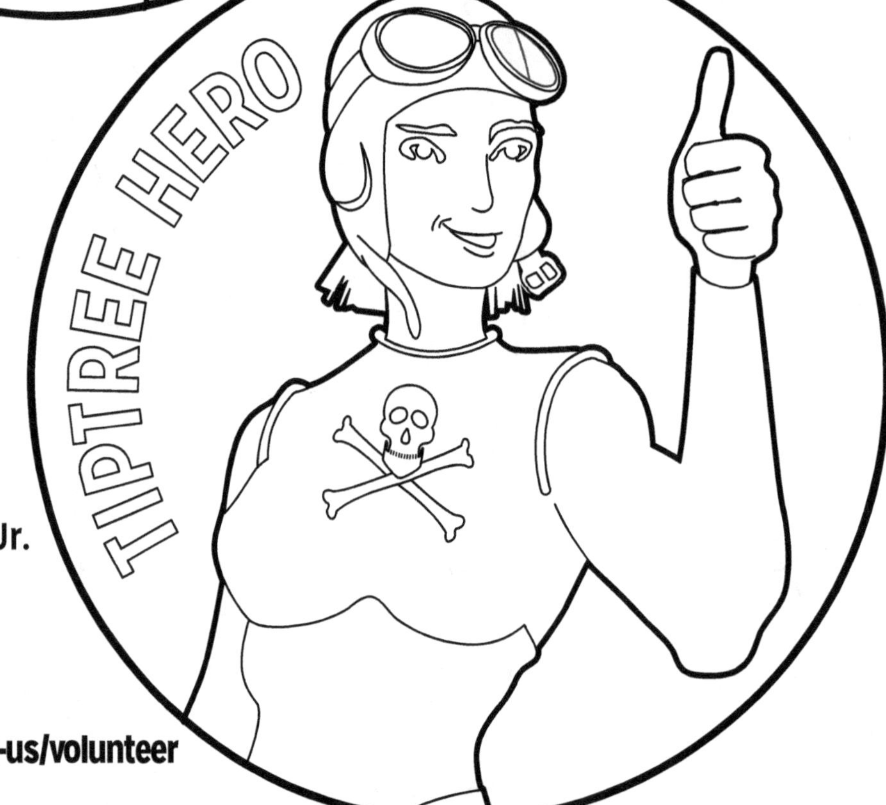

For more information about the James Tiptree Jr. Award, go to www.Tiptree.org

To volunteer, go to https://tiptree.org/support-us/volunteer

Change the world—Volunteer!

www.ingramcontent.com/pod-product-compliance
Lightning Source LLC
LaVergne TN
LVHW081425110826
845149LV00010B/1874

* 9 7 8 0 9 9 9 4 9 9 8 1 8 *